GOD'S
OTHER DOOR

AND

THE
CONTINUITY
OF
LIFE

**ARE
PRESS**

ASSOCIATION FOR
RESEARCH AND
ENLIGHTENMENT

A.R.E. PRESS ● VIRGINIA BEACH ● VIRGINIA

Copyright © 1958
by the
Association for Research and Enlightenment, Inc.
Assigned to the Edgar Cayce Foundation, 1977.
All rights reserved.

ISBN 0-87604-007-5

27th Printing, November 1997

Cover design by Cliff Selover

CONTENTS

GOD'S OTHER DOOR

Do you remember the first time you slowly turned the screw on the microscope in your high school or college laboratory? As you watched, the tiny speck of water which a moment before had been only a shiny drop, was suddenly filled with moving spots—live organisms. A strange new world was opened to you.

In like manner, a good telescope acts to extend the range of man's visual sense. Through it, too, the imagination can be fired to a greater comprehension of the tremendous reach of the universe in which we live.

In an even more exciting manner, "seeing the world" through the eyes of a psychic—a person endowed with extrasensory powers—is to become conscious of a world far more complex than that we can perceive through our five senses.

Edgar Cayce was such a psychic.

For many years, he deliberately put aside physical consciousness twice each day to try to aid individuals who sought his help. He appeared to sleep; but in and from this state of sleep, his mind seemed to be moving in levels of consciousness far beyond the range of physical awareness.

Edgar Cayce described this world he entered while asleep. He talked with its inhabitants. He related many of his experiences. Of greatest interest to the average individual, however, are his statements which link this world in which he moved to the one we will know at death. We all travel toward *God's Other Door*. As it swings open for us, will it bring nothingness or new horizons? What has it brought to those we love?

In October, 1949, *McCall's Magazine* carried an article under the title, "How Does It Feel To Die?" It was built around Sir William Osler's statement on death: "Most human beings not only die like heros, but in my wide clinical experience, die really without pain or fear. There is as much oblivion about the last hours as about the first, and therefore men fill their minds with spectres that have no reality."

Nine outstanding physicians in large American hospitals expressed agreement with Osler. Dr. H.D. Van Fleet, President of the Los Angeles Academy of Medicine, said: "I have sat with dying men of every race and creed—Hindus, Shintoists, Catholics, Protestants, Jews, Mohammedans. They died in peace. And I have found that the sweetness of death is intensified in all men by a childlike faith in their own religion. What a man may see at the point of death will probably remain an eternal mystery. But it should remain, too, a vision with no terrors for any of us."

Most of us push away thoughts of death and face them only when we must. We might well ponder this statement from the Edgar Cayce readings: "The last to be overcome is death, and the knowledge of life is the knowledge of death." (254-17)

Certainly, we can all say with Francis Bacon, "It is as natural to die as to be born." Kahlil Gibran expresses this thought beautifully in *The Prophet:* "For life and death are one, even as the river and the sea are one."

If you would turn from poetry to logic, hear Socrates. After describing the beauty of a night of dreamless sleep, he says: "Now if death is like this, I say that to die is gain; for eternity is then only a single night. But if death is the journey to another place; and there, as men say, all the dead are; what good, O my friends, can be greater than this? . . . Nay, if this be true, let me die again and again."

What Is Death?

On October 18, 1930, Edgar Cayce had an unusual dream experience while giving a reading. Upon awakening, he described this experience as follows:

I was preparing to give a reading. As I went out, I realized that I had contacted Death, as a personality, as an individual, or as a being. Realizing this, I remarked to Death: "You are not as ordinarily pictured—with a black mask or hood, or as a skeleton, or like Father Time with a sickle. Instead, you are fair, rose-cheeked, robust—and you have a pair of shears or scissors." In fact, I had to look twice at the feet or limbs, or even at the body, to see it take shape.

He replied: "Yes, Death is not what many seem to think. It is not the horrible thing which is often pictured. Just a change—just a visit. The shears or scissors are indeed the implements most representative of life and death to man. These indeed unite by dividing—and divide by uniting. The cord does not, as usually thought, extend from the center—but is broken from the head, the forehead—that soft portion we see pulsate in the infant. Hence we see old people, unbeknowing to themselves, gain strength from youth by kissing there; and youth gains wisdom by such kisses. Indeed the vibrations may be raised to such an extent as to rekindle or re-connect the cord, even as the Master did with the son of the widow of Nain. For He did not take him by the hand (which was bound to the body as was the custom of the day), but rather stroked him on the head—and the body took life of Life itself! So, you see, the silver cord may be broken—but vibration . . . " Here the dream ended.

Reflect upon the following statements:

> *For, the earth is only an atom in the universe of worlds!*
> . . . And with error entered that as called *death,* which is only a transition—or through God's other door—into that realm where the entity has builded, in its manifestations as related to the knowledge and activity respecting the law of the universal influence.
> . . . Death in the material plane is passing through the outer door into a consciousness in the material activities that partakes of what the entity, or soul, has done with its spiritual truth in its manifestations in the other sphere.
>
> 5749-3

"God's Other Door"—In this phrase may be found not just a title for this booklet, but also the basis for a new attitude toward death.

On the Other Side of the Door

Just after death occurs, there is a period of unconsciousness which may aptly be likened to a dream state from which there is a gradual awakening. The duration of this period is governed by the development of the individual.

> . . . *for thoughts are deeds,* and are children of the relation reached between the mental and the soul, and has its relation to spirit and soul's plane of existence, as they do in the physical or earth plane. What one thinks continually, they become; what one cherishes in their heart and mind they make a part of the pulsation of their heart, through their own blood cells, and build in their own physical, that which its spirit and soul must feed upon, and that with which it will be possessed, when it passes into the realm for which the other experiences of what it has gained here in the physical plane, must be used. 3744-4

This concept is expressed with additional details in the following quotation:

> When the body-physical lays aside the material body, that in the physical called soul becomes the body of the entity, and that called the superconscious the consciousness of the entity, as the subconscious is to the physical body. The subconscious [becomes] the mind or intellect of the body.
>
> 900-34

In another reading, a direct question was asked about the form of the entity after death; it was answered as follows:

> *Q-4. What form does the spirit entity take . . . ?*
> A-4. Taking that form that the entity creates for itself in the plane in which the existence is passed. As we have in the earth's plane the imagination, the mind of the individual pictures to itself, through its carnal relations, that condition to which its individual relation of entity assumes to itself, and the entity possessing that same ability to assume that position in which it may manifest itself according to its relative position to that merited condition in its existence.
>
> 900-19

We may wonder if some of the fairy tales which are part of the lore of every race were not really written about forms found in the world beyond "the other door" instead of this earth plane.

> As the soul and spirit entity takes its form in the spiritual plane, as the physical body takes form in the material plane, it is subject in the spiritual plane to those immutable laws of the spiritual plane. The spiritual entity of the individual is composed, then, of the spirit, the superconsciousness, the soul, the subconscious body, as the body is prepared for the entity in the spiritual plane, taking then the position in the universal force, or space, that the entity has prepared for itself, and goes through its development in that plane, until ready again to manifest in the flesh plane, and sow that degree of development toward that perfection that would make the entity in its entirety perfect, or one with the Creator.
>
> This is the cycle, or development, or condition, of the entity in the earth plane, and in the spiritual plane, whether

4

developed to that position to occupy that it occupies, with its relative conditions left in the environment, and giving, partaking, or assisted by such conditions in its completion of development. As this: We would find the ever-giving forces, as long as not given to becoming in that sphere that would bring the entity into the perfect conjunction with the universal force, the entity depending, whether in spiritual plane, or physical plane, upon its relation with the sphere to which it is the closer attracted. Hence we have those conditions as expressed in the earth's plane; those individuals of a spiritual nature, those individuals of the material nature; the nature not changing in its condition, save by the environment of development.   900-20

After-Death Experiences

One may conclude that it is fallacious to reduce death to a common denominator. It is a very individual, a very personal experience. Awareness in the transition period differs with each entity. Some additional differences as well as similarities may be noted in the following readings:

> Q-1. *Does death instantly end all feeling in the physical body? If not, how long can it feel?*
> A-1. This would be such a problem; dependent upon the character of which unconsciousness is produced to the physical reaction—or the manner in which the consciousness has been trained [to think about death].
> Death—as commonly spoken of—is only passing through God's other door. That there is continued consciousness is evidenced, ever, by . . . the ability of entities to project or to make impressions upon the consciousness of sensitives or the like.
> As to how long [death may take]—many an individual has remained in that called death for what ye call *years* without realizing it was dead!
> The feelings, the desires for what ye call appetites are changed, or not aware at all. The ability to communicate is that which usually disturbs or worries others.
> Then, as to how long—that depends upon the entity.
> For as has been given, the psychic forces of an entity are *constantly* active—whether the soul-entity is aware of same or not. Hence as has been the experience of many, these become as individual as individualities or personalities are themselves.

Q-2. If cremated, would the body feel it?

A-2. What body? The physical body is not the consciousness. The consciousness of the physical body is a separate
thing. There is the mental body, the physical body, the
spiritual body.

As has so oft been given, what is the builder? *Mind!* Can
you burn or cremate a mind? Can you destroy the physical
body? Yes, easily.

To be absent (what is absent?) from the body is to be
present with the Lord, or the universal consciousness, or the
ideal. Absent from what? What absent? Physical
consciousness, yes.

As to how long it requires to lose physical consciousness
depends upon how great are the *appetites* and desires of a
physical body!   1472-2

We find another reference to the differences in states of
consciousness at death in the following extracts:

*Q-5. Describe some of the planes into which entities pass
on experiencing the change called death.*

A-5. Passing from the material to a spiritual or cosmic, or
outer consciousness, oft an entity or being [does] not become
conscious of that about it; much in the same manner as an
entity born into the material plane only becomes conscious
gradually of that designated as time and space for the
material or third-dimensional plane. In the passage the
entity becomes conscious or the recognition of being in a
fourth or higher dimensional plane takes place, much in the
same way as the consciousness is gained in the material.

For, as we have given, that we see manifested in the
material plane is but a shadow of that in the spiritual plane.

In materiality we find some advance faster, some grow
stronger, some become weaklings. Until there is redemption
through the acceptance of the law (or love of God, as
manifested through the Channel or the Way), there can be
little or no development in a material or spiritual plane. But
all must pass under the rod, even as He—who entered into
materiality.   5749-3

The In-Between State

The mind is the builder, ever, whether in the spirit or in
the flesh. If one's mind is filled with those things that
bespeak of the spirit, that one becomes spiritual-minded.

6

As we find in a material world: envy, strife, selfishness, greediness, avarice are the children of *man!* Long-suffering, kindness, brotherly love, good deeds, are the children of the Spirit of Light.

Choose ye (as it has ever been given), whom ye will serve.

This is not beggaring the question! As individuals become abased, or possessed, are their thoughts guided by those in the borderland? Certainly! If allowed to be.

But he that looks within is higher, for the spirit knoweth the Spirit of its Maker . . . and "My Spirit beareth witness with thy Spirit," saith He who giveth life!   5753-1

The following extract reminds one of the layman's concept of purgatory. Notice the idea of a soul *meriting* a certain state of consciousness after death:

Q-2. Where do entities recede to after leaving earth's plane?

A-2. As was given, in that "Touch not, for I have not yet ascended unto my Father." In the separation of the soul and spirit from an earthly abode, each enter the spirit realm. When the entity has fully completed its separation, it goes to that force through which the entity merits in the action upon the earth's plane, and in the various spheres, or in the various elements, as has been prepared for its (the spiritual entity) development, so the sojourn is taken, until the entity is ready for again manifesting through the flesh that development attained in the spiritual entity, for the will *must* be made one with the Father, that we may enter into that realm of the blessed, for, as has been given, only the true, the perfect, may see God, and we *must* be one with Him.   294-15

Q-2. [Is it true] that the memory reveals itself some time after death to a spiritual-minded person, not only as related to the earthly life, or the remaining earthly thoughts of earthly life, but also reveals itself as a self-unfoldment of all past experiences?

A-2. Correct. For life, in its continuity, is that experience of the soul or entity—including its soul, its spirit, its superconscious, its subconscious, its physical consciousness, or its *material* consciousness, in that as its *development* goes through the various experiences takes on more and more that ability of knowing itself to be itself, yet a portion of the great whole, or the one Creative Energy that is in and through all.   900-426

Q-4. Does the spiritual entity, after leaving the earth's plane, have full realization of the physical life, or experience through which it passed while on earth's plane?

A-4. It may, should it so choose . . . As in this: In the way that the spiritual insight was given into the heart and soul of Saul of Tarsus, as he beheld his Master in that realm to which he had passed. The consciousness in the material world reached his consciousness of a material world, through the material consciousness of another material individual. The vision as beheld by him, in the way that of the superconsciousness manifests in his subconsciousness.

Q-5. . . . Will that full realization remain with him in the next plane, or when he leaves this earth's sphere? Will he know he was [900] on earth, an individual with definite personality and character, and will he be able to realize that which he was and that which he has become?

A-5. When he, [900], has reached the perfect realization of these consciousnesses of personae and personalities of individuals and of self (to which he may develop), he will become able to attain such superconsciousness in a spiritual plane, as has been outlined. At present, no.   900-16

Q-3. Is it the destiny of every spiritual entity to eventually become one with God?

A-3. Unless that entity wills its banishment. As is given with man, in the giving of the soul, the will, wherewith to manifest in the entity, whether spiritual, whether material. With that, the entity either spiritual or physical, may banish itself. Again a compliance with law; as has been given, Hell was prepared for Satan and his angels, yet God has not *willed* that *any* soul should perish. Giving of will to His creation, man, that man might be one with Him, giving man the privilege of exercising his (man's) will, or exercising His (God's) will to be one with Him. As in destiny, meaning a law, compliance with a law, destined to be subject, or *being* the law. The destruction of same destined to the contribution to the destruction of such law . . .

Q-5. When an entity has completed its development, such that it no longer needs to manifest on earth's plane, how far then is it along towards its complete development towards God?

A-5. Not to be given. Reach that plane, and develop in Him, for in Him the will then becomes manifest.   900-20

In the following extract we find the idea that a soul on the next plane of consciousness first takes on and then moves out of a body-like form as it progresses in its spiritual evolution. Students of Theosophy will find parallel concepts here. Notice that this material is given in answer to a question assuming a personal experience of astral projection.

> Q-5. *In regard to my first projection of myself into the astral plane, about two weeks ago: Some of the people were animated and some seemed like waxen images of themselves. What made the difference?*
>
> A-5. Some—those that appear as images—are the expressions or shells or the body of an individual that has been left when its soul self has projected on, and has not been as yet dissolved—as it were—to the realm of that activity.
>
> For what individuals are lives on and takes form in that termed by others as the astral body. The soul leaves same, and it appears as seen. Other individuals, as experienced, are in their *animated* form through their own sphere of experience at the present.
>
> Q-6. *Why did I see my father and his two brothers as young men, although I knew them when they were white-haired?*
>
> A-6. They are growing, as it were, upon the eternal plane. For, as may be experienced in every entity, a death is a birth. And those that are growing then appear in their growing state.
>
> Q-7. *Any other advice?*
>
> A-7. First, do those things that will make thine body—as it were—*whole*. Projections, inflections, astral experiences, are much harder upon those who are not *wholly* physically fit.   516-4

When asked if at death the entity became free of a physical or material body, the answer was given:

> Free of the material body but not free of matter; only changed in the form as to matter; and is just as acute to the realms of consciousness as in the physical or material or carnal body, or more so.   262-86

> . . . there is no death, only the transition from the physical to the spiritual plane. Then, as the birth into the physical

is given as the time of the new life, just so, then, in physical is the birth into the spiritual. 136-33

Summary

. . . death, as commonly viewed, is not that of the passing away, or becoming a non-entity, but the phenomenized condition in a physical world . . . 136-18

The passing in, the passing out, is as but the summer, the fall, the spring; the birth into the interim, the birth into the material. 281-16

. . . a death in the flesh is a birth into the realm of another experience, to those who have lived in such a manner as not to be bound by earthly ties. This does not mean that it does not have its own experience about the earth, but that it has lived such a *fullness* of life that it must be about its business. 989-2

. . . growth in the astral world . . . is the digesting and the building of the same oneness in the spirit, the conscious, the subconscious, the cosmic, or the astral world. 5756-4

Communication With Other Planes

In considering continuity of consciousness after death, the question of greatest interest to many people is the nature of communication between those here, and the world beyond the Other Door. Other questions that arise are, "Is it right to communicate? Is it helpful to those with whom there is communication? Should we make the attempt—and if so, when and how? And, what *kinds* of communication are there?"

It is helpful at this point to understand the source of Edgar Cayce's information. This will answer many of the questions and help enlarge the concept of life after death.

Many students of psychical research, and especially those whose personal experiences involve spiritualistic phenomena, assume that the Edgar Cayce phenomenon was of a mediumistic nature. It is not unusual to be asked: "Who was Edgar Cayce's guide or control? A group of doctors must have helped him."

Friends inclined to this point of view usually look slightly embarrassed when they hear the readings' own explanation regarding the source of the information. For, as you will see, the explanation includes that of communication with entities on other planes of consciousness—but it is not limited to such communication as the only source! (It is quite possible that many fine psychic mediums are actually limiting themselves by not recognizing their own extrasensory faculties.)

People who heard their own personal readings, as well as those who listened regularly to the daily readings for others, observed no evidence at any time that "spirit entities" took over the body and voice of Edgar Cayce. The basic qualities of his voice remained unchanged during a reading. No personality characteristic was ever shown which could not be recognized as a conscious trait. Letters and reports in the records show that many people were disappointed when they found that it would not be possible to speak with some loved one in the "spirit world," through a reading.

Many of the records of readings, however, do contain information indicating that Edgar Cayce talked with personalities on other planes of consciousness, and even transmitted their points of view. At times, those present during the reading could hear one side of a conversation between Edgar Cayce and someone who could not be seen. We shall give several extracts illustrating this type of communication.

What did the readings say was the source of information for the readings? Here is one answer, from a reading dated October, 1923:

> The information as given or obtained from this body is gathered from the sources from which the suggestion may derive its information.
>
> In this state the conscious mind becomes subjugated to the subconscious, superconscious or soul mind; and may and does communicate with like minds, and the subconscious or soul force becomes universal. From any subconscious mind information may be obtained, either from this plane or from the impressions as left by the individuals that have gone on before, as we see a mirror reflecting direct that which is before it. It is not the object itself, but that reflected as in this. The suggestion that reaches through to the subconscious or soul, in this state, gathers information from that as reflected from what has been or is called real or material, whether of the material body or of the physical forces, and just as the mirror may be waved or bended to reflect in an obtuse manner, so that suggestion to the soul forces may bend the reflection or that given; yet within, the image itself is what is reflected and not that of some other.
>
> Through the forces of the soul, through the mind of others as presented, or that have gone on before; through the

> subjugation of the physical forces in this manner, the body
> obtains the information.   3744-2

Other readings explained that the development of the entity, Edgar Cayce, took place in past lives in the earth and on "mental planes" beyond the earth's sphere of influence.

Closeness of attunement achieved for each reading was an important factor affecting the range and accuracy of the reading. Other factors affecting the clarity of focus were the desire, the need and the development of the individual seeking help through a reading.

Let's return for a moment to the illustration of the telescope. An image through the finest instrument will be only a blur if the instrument is imperfectly focused. During a reading, Edgar Cayce was tuned to the mental body as a whole. Hence the conscious, subconscious and superconscious activities of the seeker were a part of the process of focusing. To assume that this focusing was a mere mechanical process resulting from suggestion would be an over-simplification.

Neither can the influence of Edgar Cayce's *conscious mind* in focusing for any reading be ignored. He constantly tried to control his personal attitude with regard to individual readings: he made a practice of not reading questions prepared for the readings; he did not want to know anything about the person applying for the information; he insisted that each person make a personal request, because he believed that such an expression of desire helped to set up a mental bridge; and through the years he always encouraged those requesting a reading to maintain a prayerful, meditative state during the actual period of the reading.

Nevertheless, there were times when his feelings overshadowed and influenced a "reading period." Anger sometimes prevented him from laying aside consciousness to give a reading. His own readings warned him not to attempt to give information when he was ill.

This leads one to ask what took place during a reading—especially in relation to his attunement with entities having bodies different from our own.

Edgar Cayce said he could withdraw from the physical body just as one withdraws at death. Because of his development, he was then free to move through many levels of consciousness.

He could attune to the subconscious level of another living person, and from that level describe physical conditions of the body unknown to physical consciousness. He could also attune to higher levels of consciousness, to touch the aspirations, purposes and development of the soul-mind—if our life-reading reports may be considered evidence.

12

He could tune in to thought-patterns and thought-forms. It was from these general reservoirs of thought that he seemed to draw much of his general health information.

In addition, he could tune in to the minds of entities on various planes other than the earth. He describes some of these planes from a dream experience he had twelve to fifteen different times, while giving life readings. Here is one description of his dream:

I see myself as a tiny dot out of my physical body, which lies inert before me. I find myself oppressed by darkness, and there is a feeling of terrific loneliness . . . Suddenly, I am conscious of a white beam of light. As this tiny dot, I move upward following the light, knowing that I must follow it or be lost.

As I move along this path of light, I gradually become conscious of various levels upon which there is movement. Upon the first levels there are vague, horrible shapes—grotesque forms such as one sees in nightmares. As I pass on, there begin to appear on either side misshapen forms of human beings, with some part of the body magnified.

Again there is a change, and I become conscious of gray-hooded forms moving downward. Gradually these become lighter in color. Then the direction changes, and these forms move upward—and the color of the robes grows rapidly lighter.

Next, there begin to appear on each side vague outlines of houses, walls, trees, etc., but everything is motionless. As I pass on, there is more light and movement, in what appear to be normal cities and towns. With the growth of movement, I become conscious of sounds—at first indistinct rumblings, then music, laughter and the singing of birds. There is more and more light; the colors become very beautiful; and there is a blending of sound and color.

Quite suddenly, I come upon a hall of records. It is a hall without walls, without a ceiling; but I am conscious of seeing an old man who hands me a large book—a record of the individual for whom I seek information.

According to this dream, entities appear to occupy different positions on the various planes in respect to their development. A mental attunement could be set up with any of those within the range of what Edgar Cayce called "the sphere of communication." Here is further explanation of the meaning of attunement:

Q-20. Is it possible for this body, Edgar Cayce, in this state, to communicate with anyone who has passed into the spirit world?

A-20. The spirit of all that have passed from the physical plane remain about the plane until their development carry them onward or are returned for their development here; when they are in the plane of communication or remain within this sphere, any may be communicated with. There are thousands about us here at present . . .

Q-24. *To what place or state does the subconscious pass to receive this information it gives?*

A-24. Just here in the same sphere as when the spirit or soul or spirit and soul are driven or removed from the body or persons.   3744-2

Q-1. *What is meant by souls within this sphere may be communicated with by the body, Edgar Cayce, in the psychic state?*

A-1. Each and every soul entity, or earthly entity, passing through the earth's plane, radiates in that plane those conditions that are radiated from the soul or spiritual entity in the individual. This, then, becomes the fact, the real fact, in the material world. When the body, Edgar Cayce, is in the psychic or subconscious condition, he is able then to reach all subconscious minds, when directed to such subconscious minds by suggestion, whether in the material world or in the spiritual world, provided the spiritual entity has not passed entirely into that condition where the radiation, or the relative forces, are superseded by other radiations. Then we only reach those radiations left in earth's plane that are taken again when entering in earth's plane, whether entity is conscious of same or not. The consciousness of reaching that condition wherein the physical body may take up that truth known, must be reached by all. Hence the given expression that the body, Edgar Cayce, in the subconscious condition, may communicate with those passed into the spiritual plane.

Q-2. *In reality, then, the body, Edgar Cayce, in the psychic state, communicates with thoughts, and not with the spiritual entities themselves.*

A-2. With the thoughts, and with the radiation as is given. Then we have as the illustration of this condition in the body, [900]. We have, when this entity enters the subconscious, through the medium of laying aside the conscious mind, and the projection of the spiritual guide, the father, the thoughts, the impressions, as would be given by that entity, entering the subconsciousness of [900]. Not the spiritual entity's taking form, save in the subconsciousness of [900].

Q-3. Then, may the body [900]'s spiritual guide recede to that point, or position, where the body, [900], may no longer receive those radiations?

A-3. Not until [900] supersedes those radiations by creations in radiations of his own, for thoughts are deeds, and all conditions remain, as given.

Q-4. Are those radiations like a vibratory force on our earth's plane, such as light wave?

A-4. May be compared to same, but of the spiritual radiation, and not material radiation; that is, those radiations as come from spirit form may take form in vibratory radiation of color, or light, through the individual's attunement.   900-22

The Ability to Communicate

Now let us turn to a general reading given on Spirit Communication, given March 16, 1927. We come now to the answers to many personal questions.

First, let it be understood there is the pattern in the material or physical plane of every condition as exists in the cosmic or spiritual plane, for things spiritual and things material are but those same conditions raised to a different condition of the same element—for all force is as of one force.

In that period when the spirit, or when the soul (best that these be classified, that these be not misunderstood, then, in their relations one to another), is in the material, the body physically composed of the physical body, the mind, and the soul, and the subconscious mind, and the superconscious mind, or the spirit.

In the make-up of the active forces of the physical body, it (the body) is constituted of many, many, cells—each with its individual world within itself, controlled by the spirit that is everlasting, and guided by that of the soul, which is a counterpart—or the breath that makes that body individual, and when the body is changed, and this is the soul body, the elements as are patterned are of the same. That is, that builded by thought and deed becomes the active particles, atoms, that make up that soul body, see?

When the soul passes, then, from the physical body, it (the soul body) then constituted with those atoms of thought (that are mind) and are of the Creative Forces a part, and

15

then we have the soul body, with the mind, the subconscious mind, its attributes—which have been explained or given heretofore, as the relation of what the subconscious mind is—which never forgets, and is then as the conscious mind of the soul body; the spirit or superconscious mind being that as the subconscious mind of the material body—the place, then, of the resident or residence, or that occupied by the soul body becomes to the finite mind the first question. The occupancy is at once—as is seen here, there are about us many, *many, many,* soul bodies; those upon whom the thought of an individual, the whole being of an individual is attracted to, by that element of thought—just the same as the action in the material body—for remember, we are patterned, see? one as of another. In the next, then, we find that, that as *builded* by that soul is as the residence of that soul, the companion with that as has been builded by that soul—either of the earthbound or of that element or sphere, or plane, that has its attraction through that created in that soul being in the actions, by the thoughts, of that as an individual. Hence we find there are presented the same conditions in the astral or cosmic world, or cosmic consciousness, as is present in the material plane—until the consciousness of that soul has reached that development wherein such a soul is raised to that consciousness *above* the earth's sphere, or earth's attractive forces—until it reaches up, up, outward, until included in the ALL, see?

In the next step, then, we find, as regarding information given, the ability of such a body, or entity, to communicate with those in the material plane:

Question and answers are often confusing, by those that give or supply information concerning such experiences; for each experience is as individual as the individual that receives same, or the entity that transmits same, and the possibility, probability, the *ability,* of individuals to so communicate, or so draw on those forces, is raised, limited, or gained, by the act of the individual seeking its ability to so communicate—for, remembering, conditions are not changed. We find individuals at times communicative. At other times uncommunicative. There are moods, and there are moods. There are conditions in which such conditions are easily attained. There are others that are hard, as it were, to meet or cope with. The same condition remains in that distant sphere—as is felt by many—when it is the *same* sphere, *unless* the individual, or the entity, has passed on.

Then, the next question that arises is: How are such communications brought about? Just as given. When the body (material) attunes self to that plane wherein the sensuous consciousness is in obeisance to the laws of physical or material, and the spiritual or astral laws are effective, those of the astral plane may communicate, in thought, in power, in form. What form, then, do such bodies assume? The desired form as is built and made by that individual in its experience through the material plane. Remembering our pattern. We find bodies are made by the action of cell units in the material body. Some to beauty, some to distress—by that merited for the physical experience. Hence a necessity of a physical experience, that the *desires* that build may be made, changed, or acted upon.

Again we return to the astral or the soul body. In the various forms of communication, why, *why,* is such communication so often of seemingly an unnecessary nature, or seemingly inadequate to the mind of the soul entity, as understood by the mind of one hearing, seeing, or experiencing, such a communication? As may be illustrated in: The message as may be received from the boy just passed into the spirit world, and able through mediumistic forces of someone to communicate to mother, "All is well. Do not grieve. Do not long for the change." Such seems to be in the nature of rebuke to a conscious mind when momentous questions as might be propounded, could be, or would be—as some mind would say—given. Remember the pattern as is set before. Is the greeting, *in* the greeting of some profound questions the first meeting? Rather cultivate that of such communication, and receive the answer to that of the most profound that may be propounded in any way and manner to those seeking such information. Is such information always true? Always true, so far as the individual has brought self into that attunement as is necessary for the perfect understanding of same. Do not attempt to govern information, or judge information, by the incorrect law, see? When force is taken, what is the impelling force such as is seen in the movement of material objects? When under stress, the communication or the appearance of the soul body is in contact with the individual mind; such as we have seen and experienced through that of the information as has been given. Such impelling forces, we find, are the combination of that in the individual receiving and in the abilities of the individual so communicating—that is, we find that in the various experiences of individuals, levitation, or objects that are of material nature, are moved about by the active principle of the *individual through whom such manifestations are being made,* and not by spirit action, or soul action. Yet *controlled* by that cosmic consciousness. Don't leave that out, see? Controlled—for, as given, the body must be subjugated that such force may manifest. Then we see undue strength, undue power, is seen exercised at such periods. True—for things that are controlled by spirit alone are of a great deal greater active force than of the sensuous mind, as a trained mind is more active than one untrained.

Now many questions have been given. Many various forms of the active forces of communicative energies, or of soul forces, as are manifested in the spirit world and in the material world, have been given—but these as we have given here are set forth that those who would study may have the basis of an understanding that will give each and every one that knowledge that the physical world, and the cosmic world, or the astral world, are one—for the consciousness, the sensuous consciousness, is as the growth from the subconsciousness into the material world. The growth in the astral world is the growth, or the digesting and the building of that same oneness in the spirit, the conscious, the subconscious, the cosmic, or the astral world. We find, from one to another, individuals—individuals—retained in that oneness, until each is made one in the Great Whole—the Creative Energy of the Universal Forces as are ever *manifest* in the material plane.   5756-4

Summary

A summary of the above points will provide a thoughtful review:

(1) Death does not necessarily bring immediate spiritual enlightenment.
(2) Communication is controlled by attunement established on both planes. There must be a mutual desire.
(3) Much communication may take place with thought impressions.
(4) Emphasis is on the fact that the physical plane is just one level of consciousness—a part of the whole, like a room in a house.

Many people are sincerely concerned with the advisability of communication in the spirit realms—the possible harm or benefit to those in the material and other planes. The subject is discussed from many points of view in the readings quoted below.

The following reading was given for a woman whose brother was dead, and tells of help which can be given those who have passed on.

Q-1. The entity has had the experience of awaking at night and feeling the presence of her brother—would appreciate an explanation of this.

A-1. This is a reality.

Q-2. On June 2, 1942, the entity heard her brother calling her—was this the exact time that he passed on?

A-2. Not the exact time, but the time when the entity could—and found the attunement such as to speak with thee.

Q-3. Was there something he wanted her to know?

A-3. Much that he needs of thee. Forget not to pray for and with him; not seeking to hold him but that he, too, may walk the way to the light, in and through the experience. For this is well. Those who have passed on need the prayers of those who live aright. For the prayers of those who would be righteous in spirit may save many who have erred, even in the flesh.   3416-1

Q-10. [After I pass on,] could I deliver a message to [140] or my mother? Then why could not I deliver a message through another mind, another channel that I might find, to convey a message to [137]?

A-10. Only with an attunement is the message received, as in the radio. Only with the same attunement may a message be delivered to an individual, see? . . . the medium is as but that through which the transmission of a condition passes or exists, and is wavered by that physical, by that cosmic consciousness of that individual; while (get the difference, see?) a subconscious condition in which the subconscious contacts by suggestion the whole one spirit force that is, as an element of existent force in nature, and in the condition, the presentation of the fact—is manifested according to abilities of the entity to present same to the consciousness of the individual desiring that information from that cosmic consciousness, see? You don't see, but this is it, see? 140-10

Q-2. Does communication further or retard, or not affect, the spiritual progression of those in spirit life?

A-2. It does all! There are the same elements as in material; for, as *is* known, that which has materialized into matter is of the elements that are dematerializing, or dematerialized, and where aid may be lent there must be the desire. Even as seen, known, understood by many, those desires have carried an entity on to heights that are detrimental to be called into association with purely materialization, or material, for all are given to that to which they have attuned or builded, that that is of both the material and spiritual essence of truth, fact, condition, whether positive, negative, or static.   5756-8

For mind is the builder and that which we think upon may become crimes or miracles. For thoughts are things and as their currents run through the environs of an entity's experience these become barriers or stepping stones, dependent upon the manner in which these are laid as it were. For *as* the mental dwells upon these thoughts, so does it give strength, power to things that do not appear.   906-3

Hence there be many phases, many characters of the manifestation of psychic forces in the material world. There are those influences from without the veil that seek—seek— that they may find an expression, that they may still be a portion of this evolution in the earth, not considering their present estate. And these bring turmoil, strife.   1135-2

Remember the first premise, "As the tree falleth, so does it lie." If there is the desire on the part of those in the spirit or fourth dimensional plane to be communicated with, and the same element of desire is attuned from another plane, stratum, sphere or condition, then such may be done; hence, it may truly be said that *all* factors have their influence, desire the ruling one; and the desire must be attuned to the same vibration of the one in another plane, as the radio; for who of those seeking would seek His Face must know, believe, that He is, attuning their abilities, their efforts in that direction, acting, feeling, knowing that there *is* a response.   5756-8

Q-15. . . . Is every thought—say in prayer, for example, directed to or of a loved one who has passed from earth's plane by the body [*900*], *received and understood by that entity in the spirit plane?*

A-15. This must not be answered from here, for these reach to the realms of the superconscious forces, and each individual awakens to these developments in their individual self and should not be hampered, tied, wedged in by the thoughts and expressions of those through a material force.

Q-16. To what extent does a fourth and fifth dimension entity guide, control, or influence affairs of the earth?

A-16. Just as much as the individual will allow same, depending upon the individual having reached the plane wherein they may attain, gain or see, understand the plane wherein such an entity having reached that plane may communicate, give force, give enlightenment, give understanding to the one of a lower dimension, for as has been given, hard for one of one faith to understand the feelings, the intent, of one of another faith, for while each intent may be in the manner to the best of their knowledge and belief, it does not affect the real status of conditions as really exist in the various spheres, save as their co-relation have one with the other. 900-66

The readings gave this advice to one individual:

Be sincere with yourself and other outside influences, even disincarnate entities with and through whom ye may obtain much, will be sincere with you. Sincerity will drive away those that might hinder, but do not use them, do not abuse them. Know that these come to thee for aid, not to aid you. Aid them! Thus are we admonished to pray for the dead. Pray for the dead, for they only sleep—as the Lord indicated. And if we are able to attune to such, there we may help. Though we may not call back to life as the Son, we can point the way. For there's only one way. And point to that, that is safe in Him, who is the way, the truth and the light. 3657-1

Examples of Communication

In examining various kinds of communication which occurred during readings, the following one is clear-cut and contains some interesting ideas. By way of background, it should be said that Edgar and Gertrude Cayce became well acquainted with a Dr. S. Gay while living in Selma, Alabama. He was the family physician; he operated

21

on Edgar Cayce for appendicitis; he delivered the child, Edgar Evans, born to Gertrude Cayce in Selma. Dr. Gay died while the Cayces were still in Selma.

At Virginia Beach, on May 6, 1929, two readings had been given for men who were in distant cities. Gertrude Cayce had given the suggestion for Edgar Cayce to wake up, when the following voluntary reading was given in Edgar Cayce's normal speaking voice:

Here, Sister—before you change this, let me give you a little piece of advice concerning what you are working with. As there are many questions often asked you, and as you often feel others are not as considerate of the position you occupy with the Forces as are manifested through Cayce, these are the things that will possibly aid you in understanding just what takes place, and as to how you— personally—may assist or may aid the individual seeking to know that as may be helpful, beneficial to themselves or their loved ones, or where others seek to gain for themselves that same experience of the position you, yourself, now occupy in obtaining for others or for self such information.

This is the condition that is ever present when such information is obtained:

When the consciousness is laid aside, there is that which takes place much in the same manner as the spring to an automatic curtain roller. This, then, is able to be pulled down or raised up with the release of the spring. *Some* call this going into the unknown. *Some* call this spiritual, or spirit, communication. Some call it the ability to gain the force of the activities of the fourth dimension—which is *nearer* correct than any explanation that may be given. For it is the plane that is of the inter-between, or that of the borderland—which all individuals occupy through that period of gaining consciousness of that sphere they themselves occupy, until such a period or such a time that there is that joining together of such forces as may again bring that individual entity into the realm of physical experience or being.

Now each individual seeks experiences, see? Each individual must experience conditions to become aware of that being present or existent in their *own* experience, or that becomes a portion of the whole of that entity.

Then, know, whenever there is the wholehearted desire of all seeking such, there may be the perfect action of the roller or spring, or there may be the perfect application of the information that may be gained.

But Sister, know this—whenever you, yourself, are in the position of the questioner, or the one seeking to gain for another such information, call ME. I will answer. This is Gay. We are through.   538-28

This appears to be a direct-telepathic type of communication. Here, Edgar Cayce does not seem to be talking with another personality (Gay); rather, Gay's thoughts appear to be acting directly through the subconscious. It seems possible that Edgar Cayce had moved to Gay's plane of consciousness and was in direct contact, rather than that Gay had moved to Cayce's level of physical consciousness. Gay's explanation of the phenomena of the readings as "activities of the fourth dimension" also indicates a movement in consciousness.

Notice that Gay mentions rebirth. He was not known to have accepted the idea of reincarnation, and this subject was not a part of Edgar Cayce's physical consciousness until life readings began in Dayton, Ohio, years after Gay died. Here, then, is a communication dealing with ideas which were not part of an entity's thought process at death.

Gay seems aware of at least some of Gertrude Cayce's attitudes and thought patterns. Of course, this could have come from Edgar Cayce's subconscious, masquerading as Gay. It is curious, however, that Gay phrases his last suggestion as he did. When Gay knew Cayce on the earth plane, various people acted as conductors. At the time of this reading, Gertrude Cayce conducted practically all of the readings. Time seems out of focus!

Another Type of Communication

After two check-physical readings given on April 10, 1929, the following unsolicited information was given:

Now, there are many here who would speak concerning the various things we have given regarding the educational end of the institutional work. *Three* would speak concerning the varied approach, of the way that would be given by each.

As we find, Robertson would say—In the presentation of the pamphlets as lessons, the spectacular of each individual experience is an approach.

While we find Funk would say—The *reason* and the self-application would be the better approach.

While we find, as is presented by Hudson—that the *way* of individual approach is the manner that should be presented in *any* information that is given to the public, knowing that—as has so often been said—it is first to the individual, *then* to the classes, then to the masses. *Classes* would be the classification under the three heads as may be presented under the teaching or the *influence* of each of these who were teachers in their physical experience. One the wonderer, the other the student, the other the reasoner—or the exhorter. In each field there is a class. While individuals differ, let the first *principle* be the starting point—ALL IS ONE! We are through for the present. 5756-7

Here the communication is through ideas, but there is also a definite reference to personalities existing in some level or plane of consciousness. Possibly, in moving through various levels, Edgar Cayce ran into thought forms representing distinct attitudes held by these men. The relationship of these attitudes toward activities and proposed activities constitutes a different type of communication from those previously presented.

Guardian Angels

Another interesting kind of communication found in the readings involves the ancient concept of guardian angels. In a portion of an individual's reading devoted to general questions, we find the following:

> *Q-4. Who is giving this information?*
> A-4. That same that stood in the position for the entity as a guide, and an aide, and that one who may be termed the guardian of this entity's activities—Demetrius . . .
> *Q-10. What is Demetrius at present?*
> A-10. The body's guardian angel. As he stood and reasoned with Paul, again as he stood as the *aide* to Paul *in* the spirit world, *this entity* in attune *with* that *as was* given by *this* entity as the messenger in Egypt—for Demetrius *there, again,* the brother and the aide in the flesh. 311-6

It seems evident from the above that this man's guardian angel is an entity on another level of consciousness at the present, but was a brother in a prior incarnation. Ties between them lie in the mental realm and relate to ideas, ideals and purposes. This reinforces the idea that we are much more closely related to souls in the realm of the mind than we may consciously think. Such relationships would exist between entities both in and out of physical bodies. The term "angel," by the way, is used here to describe a protective soul, not a celestial being.

We have another reference to guardian angels, taken from a life reading for a soldier, left for dead on the battlefield during the First World War. He had a strange experience of being helped, which was described and explained in the reading. The admonition in the latter half of the reading referred to the individual's life work.

In the angel stooping on the field, in the walking through the garden with the shadow about same—the entity was being guided, or guarded, or protected, that that as had been promised from the foundations of the world would be to each individual, "If ye will be my people I will be thy God." He that walketh in the light, and purposes in his heart to *do, be,* that which *the* Creative Forces would *have* one be, shall *not* be *left* alone! for though he walk through the valley of the shadow of death, His arm, His hand, will direct thy ways. His rod, His staff, will comfort thee! Though they walk through green pastures, or in the ways that lead down to the sea, yet His Spirit, His arm, His face, will *comfort* thee in the *way* thou goest! When one, then, is so guarded, so guided, *indeed* for a *purpose* is one kept in the way! Be not unmindful of the necessity, then, that He that guideth shall *show* the way! *Do not* attempt with thine short hands, thine poor vision, thine hardened heart, thine encasement in *this* sphere, to not give the credit where *credit* due, nor censure where censure is due. Rather let thy yeas be yea, and thy nays be nay; for the way ye know, the *manner* ye know! *Do not* tempt the Lord, thy God!   1909-3

A Personal Communication

On July 9, 1934, Gertrude Cayce, Gladys Davis, Mildred Davis and L.B. Cayce were present to hear a check physical reading on the regular schedule of appointments. The reading was completed, and the suggestion was given for Edgar Cayce to awaken, when he began the following extemporaneous readings:

There are some here that would speak with those that are present, if they desire to so communicate with them.
Mrs. Cayce: We desire to have at this time that which would be given.
Mr. Cayce: [long pause] Don't all speak at once. [pause] Yes. I knew you would be waiting, though. Yes? Haven't

found him before? All together then now, huh? Uncle Porter, too? He was able to ease it right away, huh? *Who?* Dr. House? No. Oh, no. No, she is all right. Yes, *lots* better. Isn't giving any trouble now. Haven't seen her? Why? Where have you been? Oh. She is in another change? How long will they stay there? Oh, they don't count time like that. Oh, you do have 'em. Well, those must be pretty now, if they are all growing like that way. Yes? Yes, I'll tell her about 'em. Tell Gertrude you are all together now, huh? Uncle Porter, Dr. House, your mother? And Grandma. Oh. Grandpa still building. Oh, he made the house; yeah. Tell Tommy what? *Yes!* Lynn? Yes, he's at home. Oh, you knew that! Huh? Ain't any difference? Well, how about the weather? Oh, the weather don't affect you now. Don't change. Oh, you have what you want to—depends on where you go. Sure, then you are subject to that anyway. Little baby too! How big is it? Oh, he is *grown* now, huh? Yes. Coming back! When? Oh. Uh-huh. All right. Why? Oh yes, they hear you—I'm sure they do. *I* hear you! For Gertrude? Yes, she is here—she hears you. Oh, yes!

Mrs. C.: I don't hear. May I have the message?

Mr. C.: [continuing] Sure, she hears you; don't you hear her talking? No, I don't know what she says.

Mrs. C.: I don't hear. Will you repeat the message for me?

Mr. C.: Mama and Dr. House and Uncle Porter and the baby—we are all here. Grandpa has built the home here, and it's *nice!* And we are all waiting until you come, and we will all be here ready—we are getting along *fine,* doing *well,* yes! No. No more troubles now, for spring borders [?] all along the way; for we have reached together where we see the light and know the pathway to the Savior is along the narrow way that leads to *His* throne. We are on that plane where you have heard it spoken of that the body, the mind, are one with those things we have builded. Yes, I still play baseball, and Charlie has recently joined my club and I am still Captain to many of 'em. Well, we will be waiting for you!

5756-13

When asked who gave this information, Edgar Cayce gave the name of Mrs. Cayce's younger brother, who died many years before.

Only a few examples of this type of communication are found in the records; however, these reveal a great deal about the nature of life after death, as Edgar Cayce knew it through his daily reading periods.

Again we get a definite impression of movement on the part of some phase of Edgar Cayce's mind. For example: "I knew you would be waiting," . . . "all along the way," etc. Evidently, he stopped on the way back from the level of attunement from which the reading was given. He recognized several individuals who wished to communicate, and began a conversation with them. Those present in the room could hear only one side of the conversation; then he repeated a specific message which was given to him.

This is similar to the communication from Dr. Gay, but it contains a different kind of information about life after death. Let us examine this message carefully in the light of general statements made in the earlier section of this article.

A young man evidently continued the kind of physical activity ("I still play baseball") which he had enjoyed on earth. He died of tuberculosis, and had been forced to give up the game during the last years of his life. This brother also speaks of a home being finished by the grandfather. This home had become a symbol of family stability—a "point of return" in any time of trouble for various members of a large family. The grandfather was building it when he died, and it was added to, during the brother's lifetime, but not completed. The ardent desire of the grandfather was apparently fulfilled in the after-death plane, and his family was with him.

Notice that the young man had begun to recognize this home as a place on a path, rather than a "heaven" or stopping point. Notice the references to the weather, and a different measurement of time. The persons mentioned all died at different intervals. The baby referred to was probably Gertrude and Edgar Cayce's child who died while an infant. In this brother's mind, at least, growth had continued. Does the "coming back" refer to reincarnation? The idea of rebirth was not a point of view held by the young man when he died.

Additional information was desired regarding circumstances pertaining to this communication; so on July 17, 1934, another reading was given to obtain the information. The suggestion used and the major portion of the reading follow:

> *Mrs. C.: You will have before you the body and enquiring mind of Edgar Cayce and all present in this room, in regard to the experience following the reading Monday afternoon, July 9, 1934; explaining to us what happened—and why—at that particular time, answering the questions that may be asked.*
>
> Mr. C.:Yes, we have the body, the enquiring mind, Edgar Cayce, and those present in this room, together with the experience had by all present in the room on July 9, 1934.

In giving that which may be helpful, for the moment turn to that known by the body of self and by those present in the room respecting what is ordinarily termed spirit communication—should be (and that which has caused much of the dissension)—*soul* communication. For the soul lives on; and as conditions are only the release of the soul body from a house of clay the activities in the world of matter are only changed in their *relationships* to that which produces same and that the physical body sees in material or three-dimensional form. For words are the combination of sound. Sound is an activity of those things that produce or bring vibrations to activity to be heard, and are communicable to those of the various attunements.

Here we find, in the experience, that there were those that were in attune—through the vibrations from that sounded in the room at that particular period—and these sought, many—even many that spoke not, to communicate of themselves that there might be known not only their continued existence in a world of matter but of finer matter. As the sound of that attuned to those of the various vibrations are of its tonal or active force, it brings the variations in same—and they sought through those channels through which the soul-force of the body was passing at the particular time to produce that which would make known their presence in activity in that particular period; that although the various communications given at the time were from those thought to be dead (from the physical viewpoint) or in other realms, yet their souls, their personalities, their individualities, live on; the personalities being lost gradually in the oneness of the purpose and desire towards things that are the continual activity in a realm of whatever has been meted or measured by that builded in the individual experience. Hence communicated, as heard, through the soul forces of the body Edgar Cayce in its accord to those individualities that were attempting to make known their realm of activity in their various spheres of experiences at the time. See? Ready for questions.

Q-1. Why did we only hear one side of the conversation?

A-1. Denseness of matter to the spirit realm. All felt the presence of these influences, that attuned themselves to those activities. Spoke He, the Master, "They that have ears to hear, let them hear." There be none so deaf as those who do not *want* to hear. All could hear if they would attune themselves to the realm of the activity during such an experience.

How (some would ask) did the body, Edgar Cayce, or soul, attune self at that particular period and yet not remember in the physical consciousness that conversation had with those that approached to communicate or to tell those things that were to them, are to them, very vital in their experiences in the present plane? This, as has been given, is because the soul passes from the body into those realms from which is sought that desired to be known by the seeker. Here there was sought (this is on the 9th of July, see?) concerning the physical condition of a body that which in the material world would aid in correcting the mental and physical conditions. This realm from which such information is obtainable, as we have given, is either from those that have passed into the realm of subconscious activity or from the subconscious and superconscious activity through which information is being sought by that superconscious activity in the realm of physical forces in action. Hence why this particular body, Edgar Cayce, was able to attune self to the varied realms of activity by laying aside the physical consciousness. Then, if the body from its material and mental development were to be wholly conscious of that through which it passes in its *soul's* activity in such realms, the strain would be so great upon that which holds the mental and its applications of same in order for material activity as to become demented in its relationship. And he is thought crazy enough anyway!

So, the activities in the various realms are of such natures that they do not appeal to individuals often, as to their relationships one to another, as do the activities of this body Edgar Cayce. Hence, were these experiences such as to be wholly a portion of the material consciousness, how much greater would be the gap made; yet we find that more and more may the body Edgar Cayce grow to be more spiritual-*minded,* as it dwells upon those things that build for *constructive* forces in the experience of others; especially when and if the body is wholly cleansed from carnal influences and forces in its material activity, more and more will be the spiritualizing influences in the activities; yet the soul-*conscious* may in *any* period soar to those realms where it has been active in all those forces and relationships in a spiritual or soul world. See? For the planes (if they are called planes) that encircle the abilities for comprehension of that which is able to be or capable of being made into matter, form or activity in a material world are ever present in this soul's activity. Hence, when those that may be present at any experience are in accord with that being sought, or are so passive as to allow the various communications or activities to come through in their relationships to individuals present, or those that may be brought in association one with another, such experiences do come about. It is asked, then, through whom does the communication come? Why only one side being heard? For this was the bespeaking of the experience of the soul itself. But those present may hear, may experience, by the other activities of a material body, that it is taking place, or that the connections are made so that such communications may be had one with another.

5756-14

In the reading, this information was followed by a summary of what had already been given, combined with warnings about other members of the family. Careful study of these will provide insight into the concept of "movement in consciousness" and "attunement"— both of which describe the Edgar Cayce phenomena.

Spiritualistic Practices and Karmic Ties

Many life readings refer to past lives in which individuals were involved in spiritualistic practices which were causing confusion in their present incarnation. Here are two examples:

The entity was an aide to that stooldipper who sought to renounce, or have individuals renounce, those findings of individuals during the period. The entity lost *and* gained through this experience, in the name Alden. Through this experience the entity finds in the present a leaning towards the study of the various forms of manifestations of those who may be termed as those of familiar spirits, or those various forms of associations of ideas—whether builded from the imaginative forces or whether builded in the experience of the entity.

1909-1

One exceptional in many ways. One given to have close relation to the unseen forces as manifest in the material world. One whose latent forces ever governed by ennobling desire to self and others, yet one having many contradictory associations in its mental developments. . . . The personality then exhibited in the present from this sojourn, the seeking into the mysteries of all hidden forces, whether of spiritual or of material nature, delving into those physical manifestations of unseen forces active in the material world. . . . In the present we find the personality showing the seeking for the mysteries in nature, in physical, in the spiritual forces, and the ability to gain the close insight into such laws, and then to use this in the present plane, with the knowledge as gained through these, prepare self that these forces may manifest through the present entity, in the vision, in the hearing, in the feeling of the presence of those forces that are manifest in the physical world at the present time, taking cognizance of those conditions necessary for the better development in the present plane, and moving on to that higher realm. . . .   599-3

"The Seeking Within"

Many times, people were advised to seek within rather than to rely upon any kind of outside influence. We give two examples of such warnings, noting that in past lives these individuals may have developed the blocks which were presently bringing confusion.

> Q-2. To further my work in possible radio reception of cosmic messages, should I attempt to train myself in automatic writing, or use a medium?
> A-2. Rather than *automatic* writing or a medium, turn to the voice within! If this then finds expression in that which may be given to the self in hand, by writing, it is well; but not that the hand be guided by an influence outside of itself. For the universe, God, is within. Thou art His. Thy communion with cosmic forces of Nature, thy communion with thy Creator, is thy birthright! Be satisified with nothing less than walking with Him!   1297-1

Rather is it, then, in making application in the present, that the entity should study first in self as to the abilities of self to hold to the means, the measures, through which the activities in the present of the entity may attain to its highest ability in making manifest the spiritual truths that are becoming a portion of the entity's experience. For, as the entity has seen in the last few years or the last cycle of sojourn under the astrological as well as numerological urges, there is being awakened within self a power, an influence. *Do not* allow this to be directed by an entity that does proclaim himself or herself as *being* the guide. Why?

For, as indicated, the abilities have been such in self—and the soul development—that to call upon the Infinite is much greater, much more satisfying, much more worthwhile in the experience of an individual soul than being guided or directed merely by an entity outside of self that—*as self*—*is* being in a state of transition *or* development. There may be experiences when individual entities may proclaim or indicate their own activity by a name, but—as has ever been proclaimed—a name immediately sets metes and bounds about the abilities or the experience of development for a given period. Not that (as a very crude example) one would send for a plumber to judge a painting. One would not seek a well-digger to judge a musical interpretation. One would not seek for those merely because they had experienced a view without the development or training. But, as God's purpose is to *glorify* the individual man (or soul) in the earth, so the highest purpose of an individual soul or entity is to glorify the Creative Energy or God in the earth. Should the Maker use a gnome, a fairy, an angel, a developing entity *for* a guide, all right—for a specific direction; for He hath given His angels charge concerning thee; and *thy* god, thy face, is ever before the Throne of the Infinite.   338-3

In Book II, *A Search for God*, a reading explains various signs along the path of soul development: dreams, astrology, numerology, and guidance through communication. "Make your own approach to the Force," was the advice given. " . . . they are as but a candle that one stumbles not in the dark. But worship *not* the light of the candle; rather that to which it may guide thee in thy service" (707-2).

A strong warning was given for a man who was interested in spiritualism, who was trying to estimate the range of information possible through a reading.

> Q-13. *Is there anything the Forces would recommend for me to do?*
> A-13. Present thine self to those Forces that make for a more perfect relationship with the *living* God; *not* that of any individual's dead past! that would seek to climb up by *thine own* hard way; for, as was given, he that climbs up any other way than by the way of the Cross is a thief and a robber! So, make thine approach to that Force as manifests itself *in* the *material* world as the Son *to that* Throne, and be satisfied with none beneath *that* approach! So may the consciousness of the Christ life come into *thine* possession.
> 2897-4

In answering a question about the difference between automatic and inspirational writing, the same thought is expressed.

> As to the activities of what may be termed the channels through which individuals may receive inspirational or automatic writings, the inspirational is the greater of the activities—yet may partake of both the earth-earthly things and the heaven-heavenly things, while the automatic may partake only of that source or force which is impelling, guiding or directing. The inspirational may develop the soul of the individual, while the automatic may rarely reach beyond the force that is guiding or directing.   5752-4

In this matter, as in all others, the individual self must choose his own way. "There is set before thee this day good and evil, life and death. Choose thou," is often said in the readings.

The Question of Possession

Many people think that possession by an outside spirit is a condition pertaining exclusively to Biblical times. The readings make it clear that such is not the case, and give definite warnings to be observed. Unwise use of psychic power in past lives apparently accounts for some cases of mental confusion and serious psychic difficulties. We have tabulated eleven cases of varying difficulty, with diagnoses from the readings.

(1) 1572—Couldn't sleep; bothered by tiny dwarfs crawling all over her; while asleep, believes she is a man seeking sexual gratification; has gone to witchcraft doctors trying to get "dispossessed."
Reading: Glandular disturbance; incoordination between cerebrospinal and the sympathetic nervous system; pressures in lumbar region, in lower dorsal and brush-end of the spine, overstimulating glandular forces related to the plexus at the pubic bone itself. This condition is not possession.

(2) 4787—Hallucinations
Reading: Lesions in the pelvic area. Not possession.

(3) 1183—Questions about husband who drank heavily.

> *Q-6. What causes him to lose control of himself?*
> **A-6. Possession!**
> *Q-17. Regarding my husband, what is meant by "possession"?*
> **A-17. Means possession.**
> *Q-18. Does that mean by other entities, while under the influence of liquor?*

A-18. By others while under the influence that causes those reactions and makes for the antagonism, and the very *change* of the activities.

If there could be a sufficient period of refraining from the use of alcoholic stimulants and the diathermy electrical treatments used these would drive these conditions out!

But do not use same with the effects of alcohol in the system—it would be detrimental! 1183-3

(4) 3380—Severe headaches; unable to sleep.

Reading: Result of injury; psychological condition of an unusual nature. Here there is the attempt of possession during periods when the body relaxes.

(5) 3421—Woman described "a creature" which attacked her; as seen by clairvoyants, a huge octopus, which produced violent nerve reactions, jerking of body and severe pain. She had visited all kinds of doctors, and worked with various metaphysical organizations without obtaining relief.

We find that there has been the opening of the Lyden [Leydig?] gland, so that the kundaline forces move along the spine to the various centers that open with this attitude, or with these activities of the mental and spiritual forces of the body—much in the same manner as might be illustrated in the foetus that forms from conception. These naturally take form. Here these take form, for they have not in their inception been put to a definite use.

The psychological reaction is much like that as may be illustrated in one gaining much knowledge without making practical application of it. It then forms its own concepts.

Now we combine these two and we have that indicated here as a possession of the body; gnawing, as it were, on all of the seven centers of the body . . . 3421-1

It was advised that packs be used over the area of the ovaries, and osteopathic corrections be given over the coccyx area. The second reading indicated improvement. It also contains an interesting reference to such possession:

. . . the body allows itself to slip back into that consciousness controlled by the formation of that which is as a positive possession —but which is a creation of the own mental and physical self.
3421-2

(6) 422—Hallucinations; heard voices.

Reading: Indicated that the individual had been curious about psychic phenomena, had played with them. In another life, this entity had used occult power to control others. This might lead to possession in this life, unless corrected.

34

(7) 386—Hallucinations; heard voices; nervous speech.
Reading: Caused by shocks and suppression, from 8th to 12th year. Not possession.

(8) 3000—Woman concerned about influence trying to put her to sleep at night.
Reading: Recommended use of low electrical appliance. The influence could not work through the low electrical forces. When asked the source of this influence, the reading indicated that it resulted from attempts by others to impose themselves upon the entity. The person who received this reading also suffered from a blood deficiency.

(9) 3662—Considered a manic-depressive case; in an institution when reading was given.

> **Unless proper corrections are made, there must eventually be caused a full possession. . . . there are those pressures existing in the coccyx, and in the lower lumbar and sacral areas. That have prevented and do prevent the normal closing of the lyden gland. . . .**
> **3662-1**

(10) 5405—Mental collapse; shock treatments; insulin; institution.
Reading: Dementia praecox. No obsession, no possession.

(11) 5221—Nervousness; supersensitivity.

> *Q-3. How did I happen to pick this up?*
> **A-3. . . . the body in its study opened the centers and allowed self to become sensitive to outside influences.**
> *Q-4. What is it exactly that assails me?*
> **A-4. Outside influences. Disincarnate entities . . .   5221-1**

A consideration of even so small a number as eleven readings on possible possession reveals information that may be startling to some.

Possession is recognized as a definite possibility, and some constructive suggestions for eliminating the danger are given: the physical body should be in excellent condition and free from glandular disturbance, and free of lesions in the lower spine. The blood should be free from deficiencies, such as low hemoglobin, deficient white corpuscles, and deviation from normal sedimentation rate—all of which can be detected by one's physician. It is highly desirable that the individual not be fettered by confusion or blocks brought over from past lives in which psychic power was misused.

The readings explain the possibility of possession thus:

> When those desires have fastened such hold upon the inner being as to become a portion of the subconsciousness, those desires pass on. Such as one may have in gluttonous-ness, or in any condition that benumbs the mental forces of

the entity. For the subconscious, as given, is the storehouse of every act, thought, or deed . . . Hence the condition as is seen about such entity having passed into the spirit plane; it seeks the gratification of such through the low-minded individuals in an earth plane. For as thoughts become deeds, and as such desire is loosed in the plane, such conditions become the taking on of the entity from the sphere, as is given, in that "thoughts are deeds" and live as such.   900-20

It should also be emphasized that very similar symptoms are present during possession and during physical disturbances appearing to be possession. Notice the close relationship between the lower spinal areas and the endocrine glands (lyden and gonads) in the lower portion of the body.

Possession can evidently include not only influences from what Theosophists call the "lower astral," but also influences from thought forms created by the individual himself in this and other life experiences. A very fine line can be drawn here, and one should not jump to conclusions. Symptoms alone cannot be the basis; some of the eleven cases described above show more signs of possession than others.

In Closing

C.J. Ducasse, in *Is Life After Death Possible,** aptly states man's chief desire about life after death. He says:

" . . . for what man desires is not bare survival, but to go on living in some objective way. And this means to go on meeting new situations and, by exerting himself to deal with them, to broaden and deepen his experience and develop his latent capacities."

Information from the Edgar Cayce readings assuredly encourages thousands of people to think of life and death as just parts of a stream of experience.

Know that life is a continuous experience . . .   1824-1

Q-2. What is the spirit entity in the body, [900], and how may he develop it in the right direction?
A-2. This is only the portion that develops other than in the earth's plane. Spirit entity. For soul's development is in the earth's plane. The spirit entity is in the spirit plane.
900-16

Is Life After Death Possible, C.J. Ducasse, University of California Press, 1948.

To information from the readings which we have quoted, we could have added many *consciously* clairvoyant experiences of Edgar Cayce's life. These, too, point to worlds beyond the range of normal sense perception. Man has come to recognize the amazing subconscious control of his own body processes. In the total Universe, man is a part of an even greater whole which exerts an influence upon him, aware or unaware. To glimpse this world consciously, he must walk with the great saints and mystics of all ages.

In interpreting a dream of his own death, Edgar Cayce said:

> In this vision there enters many of those conditions that, to the material mind, are hard to be understood. Yet there is seen in same the basis of the oneness of Universal Forces that may be manifested through such psychic force.
>
> For, as it is seen, in that realm of the spiritual world there is the peace and communion of loved ones, in and from the earth's plane. Chaos does not rule, but rather that of oneness in purpose and truth. And when such unions, when such meetings, come in accord with conditions being viewed in the material world, these same influences come to assist, when allowed to, in the material plane. For, as is seen, there is given the compass to the physical being to guide him in the material condition of life.   294-74

There are many who testify to the truth of that closeness and communion.

Tomorrow, we pass through "God's Other Door."

THE CONTINUITY OF LIFE

[The lecture which follows was given by Edgar Cayce in February 1934.]

First, let us understand what we mean by certain terms that we must use. Not being a scientist, I cannot speak in a scientific way and manner. I am not an educated man, so I cannot speak in terms of a scholar. I can speak only from experience and observation, or from what I have read.

When we use the term "continuity of life," what do we mean by "life"? Do we mean that span from birth until death? Would it not be preferable to refer to life as the consciousness of existence?

With such a premise, I approach this question which has been sounded throughout the ages. It is one of the oldest questions that man has considered. If a man die, shall he live again? What is death? What comes next? All of these sound the same note. We must each answer within our own self. But this is my belief:

I believe that when God breathed into man the breath of life he became a LIVING SOUL—individual soul, if you please. The Spirit of God is life, whether in a blade of grass or in man! The soul of man is individual and lives on!

In the very first part of the Bible we find it noted that man was forbidden to partake of certain fruit in the Garden. In the partaking of that fruit he became conscious of his being, and it was sin—for he was forbidden to do it.

Then God reasoned with man that he must leave the Garden lest he partake of the tree of life and live forever. What did that mean? Just that? Or had Satan been correct when he said, "Ye shall not surely die if ye partake of this fruit"? What brought physical death to man? Error! The partaking of that which he was forbidden. Did it bring death to the soul? No! It brought death to the physical body!

Now to become conscious of our continued existence is to become righteous in ourselves. Then we may become conscious of our continued existence, whether in the physical realm, the spiritual realm, or whatever stage of development through which we may be passing from physical life unto spiritual life. As we pass through all the various stages, what are we attempting to gain? Righteousness within!

Jesus gave that if we had His consciousness within us we should become conscious, or should *know* what He has said to us from the beginning. What was the beginning with Christ? "In the beginning was the Word, and the Word was with God, and the Word was God." So were our souls in the beginning. The Master said, "Ye say that ye have Abraham for your father. I say unto you that before Abraham was I AM, and he rejoiced to see my day and he saw it and was glad!" Then many of those to whom He spoke these words walked no longer with Him, but turned away. Why? He was answering that same question which has been bothering man from the beginning: "If a man die, will he live again?" He said to Nicodemus, "Know ye not that a man must be born again?" When Nicodemus asked, "How can such things be?" He answered, "Are ye a teacher in Israel and knoweth not these things?"

What is it to know the continuity of life? It is to be righteous within, and to have the consciousness of the Christ within. For God is Life. Christ is Life, and Light unto all that seek to know Him; and without Him—is there any other way? *Is* there any other way? Not that He is the *only* way, but, "He that climbeth up some other way is a thief and a robber," to his own self! He *is* the Life. He came to represent that life, and the continuity of life is in the immortality of the soul.

Immortality of the soul is an *individual* thing. My soul is my own, with the ability to know itself to be itself, and yet *one with God.* That was the message Jesus gave to His disciples all the way through. "I of myself can do nothing," but the Life that is within—and the gift of God working in you—will make *you* conscious of *your* relationship to your Maker. How do we become conscious of our relationship with God? By living the Fruits of the Spirit! Spirit is the Life, and Light, that makes us conscious of immortality—which is the continuation of our oneness with God. If God *is* Life, we then must *be His* to *enjoy* the consciousness of being one with Him!

Continuity of Life, then, is being conscious of our oneness with God, through the channel that has been set before us by the Example that has come into the world to show us the Way of Life.

That consciousness exists after physical death has very clearly been pointed out to us in at least two ways that I should like to mention.

After Samuel passed on, Saul was still in trouble. He knew Samuel had rebuked him for the manner of life he had lived; yet he was in great distress and sought to know if Samuel would not give him another blessing—though Samuel had passed from the physical plane of existence. So Saul sought out a channel through whom he might speak to Samuel—and spoke to him! We find that Samuel's consciousness had not changed one iota by having passed to the other side, for his first worlds to Saul were along the same lines that he used while still on earth, "Why troublest thou me? Dost thou not know God has rejected thee already?"

Passing over did not automatically make Samuel know more than he knew when he was here; not a bit more; the manner of existence he had lived in this plane had only developed him just so far. What did Christ say about this? "As the tree falls, so shall it lie!" When we pass into another plane, our development *begins* right there in that plane. Just as our birth into the physical brings a gradual unfoldment and development in the physical.

Therefore I believe there is a gradual growth throughout. What is Truth? Growth! What is Life? God! The knowledge of God, then, is the growth into Life—or the *continuity of Life itself!*

We have another example of continuity pointed out to us in the parable which Christ gave of the rich man and Lazarus. They had both passed into what we call the death state, yet both were conscious. Living, then, is being conscious of your experience—or conscious of where you are!

Dives, the rich man, lifted his eyes, for he was in torment. Why was he in torment? Where was torment? What is torment? We want to have these questions answered in our own consciousness in our own figure of speech, so that we can encompass what we are talking about. We want to give things metes and bounds. We want to tag them with names, and, even so, we may not recognize them the next time someone calls those names. We have gotten names for almost everything, yet when we say a name, it even now means an entirely different thing to each one of us. It is our experience with that named which makes the difference; it is our own development. The same word may have varied meanings.

The place Dives occupied was his own building, his own development—and he was being tormented in a flame. Tormented in a flame of what? Fire? Well, he had the consciousness that it was fire, so it must have been something like it—for he wanted water to put it out!

It was a continued existence for that man, and he saw Lazarus in Abraham's bosom. He recognized Abraham, though he had never seen him. How? He recognized Lazarus, though possibly he had never paid any attention to him while on earth. How? You answer it. But he *was conscious* of the condition. He was *conscious!*

40

Most of us believe the Scripture; at least we believe what is written there is for our knowledge and our understanding. And if we follow that, we will come to a greater knowledge of Life—that is, God. We will come to a greater concept of how great Life is.

I would like to go into the subject of just how consciousness has to do with life and death—but that is reincarnation. Why are we not conscious of the continuity of life in the physical plane? Why do we not remember when we live again? We do not remember because we have not been righteous enough! Christ said that if we had His consciousness within us He would bring to our remembrance all things from the very beginning!

It once bothered me a great deal as a child that God spoke to the people in the Bible and did not speak to us. Now I believe that He does and will speak to us if we will only listen. So often we allow the desires of our physical bodies to so outweigh our desires for spiritual knowledge that we build barriers between ourselves and God. *We do it ourselves,* for "He is the same yesterday, today and forever," and He does not *will* that any should be lost. What prevents us from knowing more about Life, or God? Ourselves! Nothing can separate us from the love of God but ourselves—nothing! It is the will of man that can make him conscious of the knowledge of God and of all Life; it is the will of man that can separate him from God—because he enjoys rather the pleasures of the flesh for a season. "I will satisfy the desires of my body now, rather than listen to the voice that may be raised within."

I choose to think that each one of us has an individual soul, that there is *One* Spirit—the Spirit of God—going through each and every one, that makes each and every one of us akin—that makes all life and all nature akin; for Life in *every* form is dependent upon that force we call God. For, as matter came into being, it was permeated with the Spirit of God that gives life, with its ability to *carry itself on* and *make of itself* that which has been determined by God that it should be. Man only, who was chosen to be one with God—and a companion with Him from the beginning, chose rather to go his own way—as Adam. But He has prepared a way, through the Christ, who came into the world that we through Him might have life and have it more abundantly; that we at all periods of our development might be more conscious of the life of God that is within us. Christ Himself taught that we must test the spirits, and those who acknowledge that Jesus the Christ has come in the flesh are born of God. The Truth makes alive, and the Life makes you free.

In closing I would like to give an experience which I have had at infrequent intervals for many years, during the time when I am in the unconscious (so-called) or super-conscious state. This experience has come eight or ten times while giving life readings for individuals. I remember nothing of the reading, but have a very vivid impression of the following. This may help you to understand your own experiences.

I knew my spirit, mind or soul was separated from my body and that it was seeking information for another. I passed into outer darkness, so dark that it actually hurt—yet there was a stream of light that I knew I must follow, and nothing on either side of the light must detract from my purpose to receive for that other what it was seeking in the way of aid for itself.

As I passed along the line of light I became conscious of forms of movement crowding toward the light. Coming to the next plane (if we choose to call it such), I realized that the forms of movement or figures were taking shape as humans, but rather the exaggeration of human desires. Passing a little farther, these forms were gradually lost; still I had the consciousness that they were seeking the light—or more light. Then the figures gradually took form, continually coming toward the light.

Finally I passed through a place where individuals appeared much as they are today—men and women—but satisfied with their position. The number of individuals in this state of satisfaction continued to grow, and then there were homes and cities where they were content to continue as they were.

Still following the light, which grew stronger and stronger, I heard music in the beyond. Then there came a space where all was springtime, all was a-blossom, all was summer. Some were happy, some desired to remain, but many were pressing on and on to the place where there might be greater understanding, more light, more to be gained. Then I reached a place where I was seeking the records of the lives of people that lived in the earth.

Don't ever think that your life isn't being written in the Book of Life! I found it! I have seen it! It is being written; *YOU are the writer!* As to how close it is going to be to your Saviour and to your God, you alone can answer. You alone! It is our own soul development. It is up to us to answer.

If we would have life, if we would reach that Promised Land, if we would reach that consciousness, if we would become aware of our relationship, we must *live it here and now*—and then the next step is given to us. That has been His promise, and His promises are sure.

A.R.E. PRESS

The A.R.E. Press publishes quality books, videos, and audio-tapes meant to improve the quality of our readers' lives—personally, professionally, and spiritually. We hope our products support your endeavors to realize your career potential, to enhance your relationships, to improve your health, and to encourage you to make the changes necessary to live a loving, joyful, and fulfilling life.

For more information or to receive a free catalog, call

1-800-723-1112

Or write

A.R.E. Press
P.O. Box 656
Virginia Beach, VA 23451-0656

DISCOVER HOW THE EDGAR CAYCE MATERIAL CAN HELP YOU!

The Association for Research and Enlightenment, Inc. (A.R.E.®), was founded in 1931 by Edgar Cayce. Its international headquarters are in Virginia Beach, Virginia, where thousands of visitors come year round. Many more are helped and inspired by A.R.E.'s local activities in their own hometowns or by contact via mail (and now the Internet!) with A.R.E. headquarters.

People from all walks of life, all around the world, have discovered meaningful and life-transforming insights in the A.R.E. programs and materials, which focus on such areas as holistic health, dreams, family life, finding your best vocation, reincarnation, ESP, meditation, personal spirituality, and soul growth in small-group settings. Call us today on our toll-free number

1-800-333-4499

or

Explore our electronic visitor's center on the
INTERNET: http://www.are-cayce.com

We'll be happy to tell you more about how the work of the A.R.E. can help you!

A.R.E.
67th Street and Atlantic Avenue
P.O. Box 595
Virginia Beach, VA 23451-0595